YOUR PASSPORT TO

AUSTRALIA

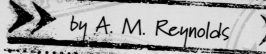

by A. M. Reynolds

CONTENT CONSULTANT

Jennifer Regan-Lefebvre, PhD
Associate Professor of History
Trinity College

CAPSTONE PRESS
a capstone imprint

Published by Capstone Press, an imprint of Capstone
1710 Roe Crest Drive, North Mankato, Minnesota 56003
capstonepub.com

Copyright © 2022 by Capstone. All rights reserved. No part of this publication may be reproduced in whole or in part, or stored in a retrieval system, or transmitted in any form or by any means, electronic, mechanical, photocopying, recording, or otherwise, without written permission of the publisher.

Library of Congress Cataloging-in-Publication Data is available on the Library of Congress website
ISBN: 9781663959256 (hardcover)
ISBN: 9781666321760 (paperback)
ISBN: 9781666321777 (ebook PDF)

Summary: Explore the sights, traditions, and daily lives of the people of Australia! Learn about the customs, traditions, food, celebrations, and landmarks that distinguish Australia from other countries.

Editorial Credits
Editor: Marie Pearson; Designer: Colleen McLaren; Production Specialists: Christine Ha and Laura Manthe

Image Credits
Getty Images: davidf, 25, GEOLEE, 19; Newscom: Morgan Hancock/Action Plus, 27; Red Line Editorial, 5; Shutterstock: Alizada Studios, 16, f11photo, Cover, Filip Bjorkman, Cover, Flipser, (passport) design element, Gordon Bell, 7, Matthew Seah, 14, Michael Leslie, 22, MicroOne, (visa stamps) design element, Oleg Bezrukov, Cover, Philip Schubert, 23, Pics by Nick, 9, pingebat, (stamps) design element, superjoseph, 13, Taras Vyshnya, 21, Tooykrub, 15, worldswildlifewonders, 17, Yevhenii Dubinko, (stamps) design element

All internet sites appearing in back matter were available and accurate when this book was sent to press.

CONTENTS

Words in **bold** are in the glossary.

CHAPTER ONE

WELCOME TO AUSTRALIA!

The sun shines overhead. The sky is bright blue. A huge rock glows red. This is Uluru, the world's largest **monolith**. It is about 500 million years old. The Anangu, a First Nation, regards it as a sacred site. Today, people from all around the world come to central Australia to see it.

Australia is an island continent. It is also a country. It lies between the South Pacific and Indian Oceans. Australia is nearly the same land size as the United States, but it has a much smaller population. The center of the country has few people. It is called the outback. The outback is mostly desert. Australia has long stretches of white sandy beaches on the coast. There are mountain ranges and dense rain forests. The country is home to many amazing animals.

MAP OF AUSTRALIA

Torres Strait

Kakadu National Park

Great Barrier Reef

Uluru

Perth

Mount Kosciuszko

Sydney

CANBERRA

Australian Alps

N
W E
S

■ Capital City   ▲ Landmark
● City   ★ Park

Explore Australia's cities, parks, and landmarks.

FACT FILE

OFFICIAL NAME: COMMONWEALTH OF AUSTRALIA

POPULATION: 25,809,973

LAND AREA: 2,966,153 SQ. MI. (7,682,300 SQ KM)

CAPITAL: CANBERRA

MONEY: AUSTRALIAN DOLLAR

GOVERNMENT: **Federal** parliamentary democracy under a constitutional monarchy

LANGUAGE: English, more than 250 indigenous languages

GEOGRAPHY: Australia is an island continent with most people living on the coast. It has many deserts in the center.

NATURAL RESOURCES: Australia has iron ore, coal, natural gas, copper and other metals, and diamonds.

PEOPLE AND LANGUAGES

Few Australians live in the outback. Most live on the coast in cities. More than 30 percent of the population was born in other countries. English is the main language. More than 300 different languages are spoken. These languages include Arabic, Greek, Mandarin, and Spanish.

Many people in Australia live in cities, including Melbourne.

The languages of the First Nations peoples are linked to the land. These people include Aboriginal people. They were the first people on the mainland. First Nations peoples also include Torres Strait Islanders. They were the first people on the Torres Strait islands.

G'DAY TO AUSTRALIA

Australians speak English. They also have their own unique words. *Ace* means "great." *Bathers* refers to a swimsuit. *Brolly* means "umbrella." And *dunny* means "toilet."

CHAPTER TWO

HISTORY OF AUSTRALIA

First Nations people teach that they have been in Australia from the beginning of time. Scientists think the first people arrived in Australia more than 65,000 years ago. Prior to the arrival of Europeans, many nations lived in a way that took care of the land. They still have strong cultural traditions.

EUROPEANS ARRIVE

Englishman James Cook arrived in 1770. Britain took Australia from the First Nations people. The British government decided to build a prison settlement. The first **convicts** arrived in 1788. The convicts worked on farms, built roads and buildings, and acted as servants. Some buildings and bridges built by convicts still stand today.

Painting has long been an important part of First Nations cultures.

In 1851, gold was discovered in Australia. More than 500,000 people from around the world rushed to Australia over the next year. Most did not find gold.

BECOMING A NATION

In the 1800s, Australia was six separate British colonies. By the late 1800s, many people believed Australia should be one nation. Each colony held a **referendum**. The people voted to unite. On January 1, 1901, Australia became one nation. It was called the Commonwealth of Australia. The British monarch remains the Australian head of state.

THE STOLEN GENERATION

From 1910 to the 1960s, many white Australians thought that First Nations people should follow white culture. The government took many First Nations children from their families. White families adopted the children. These children missed their birth families. They didn't get to learn about First Nations cultures. The children are called the Stolen Generation. In 2008, the prime minister apologized to them.

TIMELINE OF AUSTRALIAN HISTORY

65,000 YEARS AGO: First Nations people are living in Australia.

1606 CE: Willem Janszoon is the first European to map part of the Australian coast.

1770: James Cook, captain of HMB *Endeavour*, claims Australia for the British Crown.

1788: The British government forms a convict settlement in Sydney Cove.

1802–1803: Matthew Flinders sails around the continent and names it Australia.

1851: Gold is discovered near Bathurst in New South Wales.

JANUARY 1901: Australia becomes a nation.

1927: Australia's parliament moves from Melbourne to the newly built capital city of Canberra.

1939: Australia enters World War II (1939–1945).

1962: First Nations people and Torres Strait Island people are given voting rights.

2000: Sydney hosts the Summer Olympics.

2010: Julia Gillard becomes the first female prime minister.

For a long time, restrictions kept First Nations people from voting. In 1962, a new law was made. It gave all First Nations people the ability to vote in federal elections.

In 2010, Julia Gillard made history. She became the first female prime minister of Australia. Gillard was prime minister until 2013.

CHAPTER THREE

EXPLORE AUSTRALIA

The northern area of Australia is called the Top End. It is very hot and steamy. The southern states are much cooler. Snow covers the southeastern Australian Alps in winter.

Australia is full of natural beauty. The Great Barrier Reef lies along the northeast coast. It is the largest coral reef in the world. Colorful tropical fish live there. People snorkel and scuba dive in the warm water.

Kakadu National Park is in northern Australia. It has rock paintings that are 20,000 years old. There are rivers and waterfalls. Summer is the rainy season. Up to 4.9 feet (1.5 meters) of rain falls. Kakadu is home to more than 10,000 saltwater crocodiles.

FACT

Saltwater crocodiles have 64 to 68 sharp teeth. When a crocodile loses a tooth, it grows another one.

The Great Barrier Reef
makes beautiful patterns
in the ocean when
viewed from above.

Some people enjoy hiking
Mount Kosciuszko.

The Great Dividing Range is a mountain range.
It runs along the east coast of Australia through
Queensland, New South Wales, and Victoria. The
highest point is Mount Kosciuszko at 7,310 feet
(2,228 m). There are many beautiful places to visit.
Some people like to hike and stay in the mountains.

HUMAN-BUILT WONDERS

The Sydney Opera House is a famous building. It
is shaped like the sails of a ship. American singer Paul
Robeson was the first person to perform there. He
sang to the construction workers building it in 1960.

The Sydney Opera House hosts many events, including concerts, theater performances, and film showings.

The Sydney Harbour Bridge is called the Coat Hanger because of its shape. Cars, trains, bicyclists, and pedestrians use this bridge. Visitors can climb up 1,332 steps to the top of the arch.

A joey rides on its mother's back.

AMAZING ANIMALS

Australia is full of unique animals. It has about 100 species of **venomous** snakes. They typically avoid people.

Koalas live mainly in eucalyptus trees. They eat the leaves. Koalas look like little bears, but they are **marsupials**. Their babies are called joeys. A joey lives in its mother's belly pouch. When the joey grows bigger, it rides on its mother's back.

Platypuses are good swimmers.

The platypus is an unusual mammal. Its tail is like a beaver's tail. It has webbed feet and a bill like a duck. It also lays eggs. The platypus lives along rivers and streams. A baby platypus is called a puggle.

Kangaroos can reach about 6 feet (1.8 m) tall or more. Their big back feet and strong, muscular tails help them hop as fast as 40 miles (65 kilometers) per hour. A kangaroo can leap 30 feet (9 m) in one jump. This is longer than five adult humans lying head to toe.

CHAPTER FOUR

DAILY LIFE

Most Australians live in cities near the coast. People from more than 190 countries call Australia home. Australians enjoy food from many cultures. Pizza, curry, and hamburgers are very popular. At one time, **drovers** roamed the outback. They made a type of bread called damper. They used flour, water, and salt. They cooked damper in the ashes of a campfire.

FACT

In Australia, people ask for a hamburger with the lot. This includes a beef patty, pineapple, a fried egg, lettuce, bacon, tomato, and a big slice of pickled beet.

EDUCATION

Many children in Australia go to public schools. Others attend private schools. Children go to primary school and then secondary or high school. They have a long vacation over January. This is summer in Australia.

Australians enjoy a variety of toppings on their burgers.

SMASHED AVO TOAST

Smashed avo (avocado) toast is a very popular Australian breakfast food.

Toast Ingredients:
- 1 slice of thickly cut toast. Sourdough is commonly used.
- ½ avocado with pit removed
- Salt and pepper
- ½ lemon

Toast Directions:
1. Toast the bread.
2. While the bread is toasting, place the avocado in a bowl. Smash it with a fork until it is lumpy.
3. Add a pinch of salt and pepper and mix it in.
4. Pile smashed avocado on top of the toast. Squeeze lemon juice over the top.

WORK

Australians work in many industries. These include tourism, retail, mining, farming, and service industries.

People have mined in Australia for more than 150 years. The country is one of the world's leading producers of bauxite (aluminum ore), iron ore, lithium, gold, lead, zinc, diamonds, and opals.

There are several gold mines near the city of Kalgoorlie.

Miners work very hard. They often work 12 hours a day for two weeks. They then have a one-week vacation.

FACT

Miners in Victoria discovered the biggest gold nugget ever found. They dug it up in 1869. It weighed more than 159 pounds (72 kilograms).

The Royal Flying Doctor Service helps people in remote places.

Most doctors work in clinics and hospitals. But some work in planes. The Royal Flying Doctor Service helps someone every two minutes of every day. The doctors fly in small planes to isolated areas. They often use gravel driveways or highways as landing strips.

VACATIONS

Australians call vacations holidays. Beaches are popular vacation spots. People swim, snorkel, sail, fish, and surf. There are more than 10,000 beaches.

There are many beautiful places to camp in Australia.

Camping in tents and motorhomes is very popular. People set up near beaches or in the bush, which is a term for the countryside. Some people like to sleep outside under the stars. They use a swag. This is a sleeping mattress with a tentlike covering.

CHAPTER FIVE

HOLIDAYS AND CELEBRATIONS

Schools and workplaces close on public holidays. Australians love to get together with friends and family. Many people have barbecues. They cook snags (sausages) and add dead horse (tomato sauce). Anzac Day is on April 25. Australians remember those who lost their lives at war.

CHRISTMAS

Many Australians celebrate the Christian holiday of Christmas. Christmas is on December 25. Families get together. Children leave out empty pillowcases on Christmas Eve hoping they will be filled with presents. On Christmas Day, people give one another presents. They eat prawns, crayfish, roast turkey, and plum pudding for lunch.

Families enjoy outdoor barbecues on Anzac Day.

CHAPTER SIX

SPORTS AND RECREATION

Australians love to play and watch sports. One popular **spectator** sport is Australian Rules football. This game is played with an oval ball during the cooler months. The oval-shaped playing field has four poles at each end. The players try to kick the football between the two middle poles to score points. The team with the most points wins.

People play cricket over the summer. This game is played with a bat and ball. There are two teams of 11 players. Some versions of cricket last a few hours. In others, a match can last for five days.

Many children and adults play tennis. Every year, Melbourne hosts the Australian Open. This is one of the largest tennis tournaments in the world. It is one of the four Grand Slam tournaments.

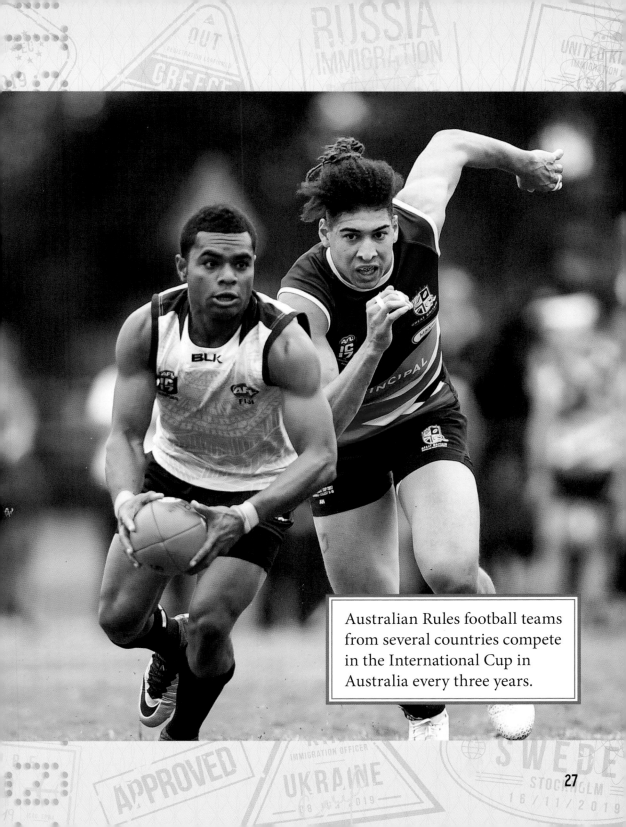

Australian Rules football teams from several countries compete in the International Cup in Australia every three years.

BACKYARD CRICKET

Backyard cricket is a popular family game. People can make it as simple as they like. Two teams of at least two players each are needed. Players will need one cricket bat or baseball bat, a tennis ball, and two sets of wickets. Upside-down trash bins or buckets can also be used as wickets. Place wickets 26 feet (8 m) apart.

1. Set boundaries behind each wicket.
2. One team will be the batters. The other team will be the bowler and fielders. Fielders stand behind the bowler and try to catch the ball.
3. The batter stands in front of a wicket. The bowler stands behind the opposite wicket. The second batter stands by this wicket too.
4. The bowler throws the ball to the batter. The batter hits the ball and runs to the opposite wicket. The second batter runs to the batter's wicket at the same time. This player will bat if the first batter scores only one run. If the first batter reaches the other wicket, the batter scores a run. The first batter can run back to the other wicket if there is time for another point. Hitting the ball over the far boundary counts for six runs. The batter does not score if the bowler hits the wicket with the ball before the batter arrives safely or if a fielder catches the ball before it bounces.
5. Repeat with the second batter and any other batters on the team.
6. After six bowls, the teams switch places. The batters become the fielders and bowler.
7. The team with the most runs in an agreed-upon period of time wins.

Swimming is very popular. Australia has won many medals for swimming at the Olympic Games. Australian beaches are not always safe. There can be big waves and sharks. Lifeguards put up flags on the beach to show where it is safe to swim.

ENTERTAINMENT

The Melbourne Cup is a horse race on the first Tuesday in November. People from all over Australia stop what they are doing to watch. Racegoers dress up in fancy hats and clothes.

FACT

The freestyle stroke is also known as the Australian crawl. This swimming style was developed in Australia.

Cities have a lot of fun things to do. People enjoy theater and live music in Sydney. Perth has beautiful swimming beaches. People can cool off in the water. They can enjoy a beachside meal. There's plenty to see and do in Australia.

GLOSSARY

convict (KAHN-vikt)
someone a court has declared guilty of a crime

drover (DROH-vur)
somebody who moves a herd of sheep or cattle

federal (FED-ur-uhl)
relating to a national government

marsupial (mar-SOO-pee-uhl)
a mammal that carries babies in a pouch on the abdomen

monolith (MAH-nuh-lith)
a single massive stone or rock

referendum (ref-uh-REN-dum)
an event where people vote for or against a particular issue

spectator (SPEK-tay-tur)
a person who watches an event

venomous (VEN-uh-muhs)
able to inject poison

READ MORE

Cronin, Leonard. *The Australian Animal Atlas.* Crows Nest, New South Wales: Allen & Unwin Children, 2017.

Golkar, Golriz. *Bindi Irwin.* North Mankato, MN: Capstone, 2019.

Somervill, Barbara A. *Australia and Oceania.* New York: Children's Press, 2019.

INTERNET SITES

DK Find Out!: Marsupials
dkfindout.com/us/animals-and-nature/mammals/marsupials/

National Geographic Kids: Australia
kids.nationalgeographic.com/explore/countries/australia/

Wonderopolis: Have You Ever Played Cricket?
wonderopolis.org/index.php/wonder/have-you-ever-played
-cricket

INDEX

ABOUT THE AUTHOR

Alison Reynolds is the author of more than 100 fiction and nonfiction books for children. She loves to share her enthusiasm for reading and writing with others. Alison lives by the sea in Australia with her husband and Rosie the dog, who has the waggiest tail ever.

OTHER BOOKS IN THIS SERIES

YOUR PASSPORT TO ARGENTINA
YOUR PASSPORT TO CHINA
YOUR PASSPORT TO ECUADOR
YOUR PASSPORT TO EGYPT
YOUR PASSPORT TO EL SALVADOR
YOUR PASSPORT TO ENGLAND
YOUR PASSPORT TO ETHIOPIA
YOUR PASSPORT TO FRANCE
YOUR PASSPORT TO GUATEMALA
YOUR PASSPORT TO IRAN

YOUR PASSPORT TO ITALY
YOUR PASSPORT TO KENYA
YOUR PASSPORT TO MEXICO
YOUR PASSPORT TO PERU
YOUR PASSPORT TO RUSSIA
YOUR PASSPORT TO SOUTH KOREA
YOUR PASSPORT TO SPAIN
YOUR PASSPORT TO SRI LANKA
YOUR PASSPORT TO TURKEY

WITHDRAWN

Anne Arundel Co. Public Library